A New True Book

PETS

By Illa Podendorf

This "true book" was prepared
under the direction of
Illa Podendorf,
formerly with the Laboratory School,
University of Chicago

 CHILDRENS PRESS, CHICAGO

Boy with toad

PHOTO CREDITS

James P. Rowan—4, 8, 10, 17, 23 (bottom), 24, 26, 27, 28, 33, 34, 43 (top left and bottom left)

Art Thoma Photos—14, 36, 37, 41 (top right)

Richard Brucher—7,8

Bobbie Lieberman (Equus Magazine)—38, 43 (middle at bottom)

Lynn M. Stone—Cover, 2, 12, 13, 19, 21, 23 (top left left and right), 28 (top right) 30, 32, 43 (top right and bottom right)

American Kennel Club (AKC)—39, 40 (top left), 41 (left, right bottom) 42

Candee & Associates—40 (left bottom)

Julie O'Neil—40 (right)

Cover—Angora Hamster

Library of Congress Cataloging in Publication Data

Podendorf, Illa.
   Pets.

   (A New true book)
   Previously published as: The true book
of pets. 1954.
   Summary: Briefly discusses the character-
istics and care of such pets as goldfish,
frogs, toads, turtles, parakeets, hamsters,
rabbits, cats, and dogs.
   1. Pets—Juvenile literature. [1. Pets]
I. Title.
SF416.2.P63   1981   636.08'87   81-7679
ISBN 0-516-01641-5   AACR2

9 10 11 12 13 14 15 16 17 R 93 92 91

TABLE OF CONTENTS

Goldfish

WHAT PETS NEED

A pet is a living animal. All pets need good care.

A pet needs food. It needs water. It needs a good place to rest or sleep.

GOLDFISH

Goldfish live in water.

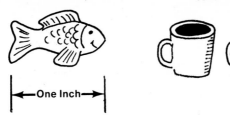 

One Inch

A fish this long needs
four cups of water. How
long is the fish?

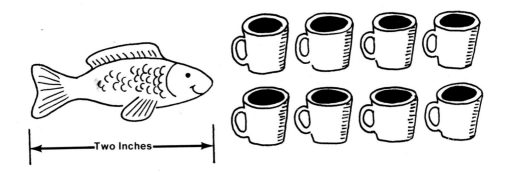

Two Inches

A fish this long needs
how many cups of water?
How long is the fish? Did
you say it needs eight
cups of water?

Angelfish

The water must be fresh and clean. Some green plants growing in the water will help keep it that way.

All fish have fins and gills.

They swim with their fins. Their tail fin helps guide them in the water.

Neon Tetra

Goldfish

They breathe underwater with their gills. Their gills have a covering over them. The covering protects them.

Fish have no ears. Their bodies take sounds from the water.

Goldfish sometimes swim to the side of the bowl when you tap on it.

Goldfish swim to the top of the water when food is dropped there.

Feed goldfish about every other day. They will die if fed too much or not enough.

Feed them just enough so that they eat it up quickly.

TOADS AND FROGS

A pet toad may be kept
in a garden or in a box.
Put damp earth about as
deep as the toad is long
in the box. Sprinkle the
earth with water to keep it
damp.

Toads eat insects and worms. Sometimes they will eat tiny pieces of fresh meat if it is dangled in front of them.

A toad looks a little like a frog.

They are about the same size.

They are about the same shape.

They take water through their skin.

They both live part of
their lives in water and
part of their lives on land.
A toad is rough and
brown. A frog is smooth
and green.

Toad

Frog

Both of them catch insects with their long tongues.

A toad can jump far but not as far as a frog can jump.

A toad can live longer out of water than a frog.

13

You can hold toads and frogs in your hands. They will not harm you.

They will not give you warts.

Toads are easy to hold because they are rough. A frog may slip out óf your hands because it is smooth and wet.

The mother toad lays eggs in water. The eggs hatch into tiny black tadpoles.

Toad eggs

Tadpoles have gills like fish. They eat plants. Back legs begin to grow. Front legs grow.

The tail becomes shorter and shorter. The tadpole becomes a little toad. It has lungs instead of gills. It lives on land. Now it eats insects, not plants.

Tadpole

Frogs are tadpoles at one time, too. Frogs grow up in much the same way as toads do. It takes some kinds of frogs two years to grow up.

TURTLES

Turtles are called "reptiles." They are called reptiles because they have scales and lungs. All reptiles have scales and lungs.

Sometimes we say turtles carry their houses with them. The houses are shells made of scales.

Painted turtle

A turtle pulls its head
and legs inside the shell.
Painted turtles live in
water. They come to the
top of the water to get air.
They can swallow food
only when their heads are
under water.

Painted turtles eat worms, lettuce, fresh chopped meat, and turtle food which we buy.

Painted turtles are easy-to-care-for pets.

The home for a pet painted turtle should have two inches of sand or dirt in it.

Painted turtle

The home should also
have about three inches of
water in it. There should
be a stone for the turtle to
crawl upon.

The sides of the home should be much higher than the turtle. Then it cannot crawl out.

A mother turtle may lay eggs in the sand or dirt. Heat from the sun will hatch the eggs.

When it is cold, the pet turtle may bury itself in the sand or dirt. It may stay there all winter. Then we say it "hibernates."

Ornate box turtle

Box turtle

There are many kinds of turtles. Box turtles are land turtles. They make good pets.

Not all kinds of turtles make good pets.

Snapping turtles do not make good pets.

A
parakeet
named
"George"

PARAKEETS

Parakeets are beautiful
birds. Some have blue
feathers. Others have
green or yellow feathers.
Only birds have feathers.

Parakeets make interesting pets. With long, patient work, you can teach a parakeet to say words.

Some parakeets make sounds like words. They may say sentences. One parakeet was taught to say, "Canaries are cute, but they can't talk."

A parakeet needs swings and other playthings in its cage.

The bird should be let out of its cage to use its wings.

A parakeet is a friendly bird. It will land on your shoulder. It will come to your finger.

Clean the parakeet's
cage every day. And give
it fresh food and water. It
should have grit in its
cage all the time.

Dwarf hamster

Angora hamster

HAMSTERS

Hamsters have soft, golden-brown fur. Animals that have fur are "mammals."

Hamsters are clean, friendly little animals. They move fast when they are awake. But they do most of their sleeping in the daytime.

Hamsters have sharp gnawing teeth.

They have a pocket in each cheek. They carry food in their pockets. When the pockets are full they empty them.

Hamsters store food in their cages.

They eat many kinds of seeds. They eat sunflower seeds when they have them. They eat carrots and apples, too.

Their cage must be made out of wire so they cannot gnaw out of it.

Mother hamsters have eight or more babies at a time. The babies are no bigger than your finger. They are pink and have no hair.

The mother may have another family in about six weeks. She may be a grandmother by the time she is four months old.

Mother hamsters take good care of their babies. The babies drink their mother's milk.

The mothers make nests for the babies out of paper and rags.

RABBITS

Pet rabbits are soft and quiet.

One pet rabbit was big and white. It had pink eyes.

It lived in a schoolroom. The children called it "Marshmallow."

Its home was a cage.
But sometimes it hopped
freely around the room.
Not all pet rabbits are
white like Marshmallow.

All rabbits eat green
grass, carrots, lettuce, or
rabbit food you can buy.

All rabbits have soft fur.
Baby rabbits have soft fur,
too. They drink their
mother's milk. When they
are old enough they eat
the same kind of food
their mother does.

CATS

Cats make fine, friendly
pets. They can learn their
names. Some cats come
when they are called.

Farmers have cats to
help catch rats and mice.
    A cat needs a warm, dry
box for a bed.
    What is the cat in the
picture doing?

Kittens are playful.

Milk, cream, fish, liver, and canned cat food are good foods for a cat.

There are many kinds of cats.

All of them have fur and feed their babies milk.

DOGS

Dogs can become good friends to their owners.

Some dogs can learn to do tricks. Some dogs can be taught to work.

Some dogs help hunters. What is the dog in the picture above doing?

Pekingese

AKC/Marian E. Hoyt

Saint Bernard

German Shepherd

Some dogs trail animals.
Some dogs help guard
the house. Some dogs are
useful only as pets.

40

Yorkshire terrier

Bloodhound

Briardale

All dogs have fur. All puppies drink their mother's milk.

There are many dog shows every year.

Dogs are trained to walk and stand as they should.

Dogs are made to look their best before they go to a dog show.

The best dog of each kind wins a ribbon.

Miniature poodles

AKC/Frances Clark, Tulsa

Piglets

Garter snake

Guinea pigs

Horse

Macaw

OTHER KINDS OF PETS

Here are some other
kinds of animals that make
good pets.

Three are like hamsters, rabbits, cats, and dogs. Do you know how they are like them? Is it the fur? Is it because the babies drink their mother's milk?

Two of these five animals do not have fur. They do not feed their babies milk.

Do you know which two they are?

The answers to these questions are on page 46.

THINGS TO REMEMBER

Pets need the right kind of food.

They need fresh water.

They need the right kind of place to rest or sleep.

Their beds and cages must be kept clean.

All pets need kindness.

These are the answers to the questions on page 44.

The piglets, guinea pigs, and horse have fur and drink milk.

The garter snake and macaw do not have fur or drink milk.

WORDS YOU SHOULD KNOW

damp—being a little wet; moist

dangle (DANG • ull)—to hang loosely

earth—soil; dirt

fin—body part of a fish used in swimming

fresh (FREHSH)—new; not stale

gill—body part of fish and other water animals used in breathing

gnaw(NAW)—chew

grit (GRIHT)—tiny, rough pieces of sand and stone

guard (GARD)—to keep safe; protect

guide (GIDE)—to show the way

hibernate (HI • ber • nate)—for animals to spend time at rest during the winter

insects (IN • sekts)—animals that have six legs and three body parts

lung—the part of the body that is used for breathing

mammal (MAM • ill)—a group of animals that is covered with fur or hair

patient (PAY • shunt)—to wait quietly; to put up with without getting angry

reptile (REHP • tile)—a group of animals that includes snakes, turtles, crocodiles, and alligators

rough (RUFF)—not even; not smooth

scale(SKAYL)—the skin that covers fish and reptiles

smooth (sMOOth)—even; not rough

sprinkle (SPRING • kill)—to scatter small drops; let fall in drops

swallow (SWAHL • oh)—to take food from the mouth to the stomach

tadpole (TAD • pohl)—a frog or toad that has just hatched

trail(TRAYL)—to follow

wart (WORT)—a small, hard lump found on the skin

INDEX

About the author

Born in Iowa, Illa Podendorf was Head of the Science Department, Laboratory School, at the University of Chicago. A pioneer in creative teaching, Illa has been especially successful working with the gifted child.